Earning High Yield in a
Low Yield World

Earning High Yield in a Low Yield World

◆

Your Guide to Understanding California Mortgage Pools

Martin I. Goodman, Founder
Residential Capital Mortgage Income Fund, LLC
www.ResCapFunds.com

iUniverse, Inc.
New York Lincoln Shanghai

Earning High Yield in a Low Yield World
Your Guide to Understanding California Mortgage Pools

iUniverse books may be ordered through booksellers or by contacting:

iUniverse
2021 Pine Lake Road, Suite 100
Lincoln, NE 68512
www.iuniverse.com
1-800-Authors (1-800-288-4677)

ISBN-13: 978-0-595-39084-7 (pbk)
ISBN-13: 978-0-595-83473-0 (ebk)
ISBN-10: 0-595-39084-6 (pbk)
ISBN-10: 0-595-83473-6 (ebk)

Printed in the United States of America

Disclaimer

The content of this publication is intended solely to provide general information about investing in mortgage pools. The information set forth herein is not intended to create, and receipt of it does not create, an offer or a contract between the recipient and the author, Residential Capital Mortgage Income Fund, LLC (the "Fund"), or their respective employees, agents, representatives or affiliated entities. Additional facts and future developments in the law may affect the subjects contained herein and no guarantee is given that the information provided is correct, complete or up-to-date. Neither the author, the Fund, nor any of their respective employees, agents, representatives or affiliated entities are lawyers or accountants, and the content of this publication does not constitute, and should not be relied upon, as legal or tax advice. For specific legal and/or tax assistance, you should consult with a licensed attorney and accountant. All uses of this publication, other than for personal uses, are prohibited.

The information set forth herein is further qualified in its entirety by the Fund's offering circular and any supplements thereto, and neither the SEC nor any state securities commission has approved or disapproved of the shares in the Fund or passed upon the adequacy of such offering circular."

Contents

Acknowledgments

There are so many people to thank who have been very supportive.

The people I work with every day are a special group of dedicated professionals working to better people's lives. Thank you especially to Lynn and Debbie for the generous feedback provided on this book.

My trusted attorneys, accountants and advisors Paul, Mike W., Mike S., Nick, Julie, Dale, Dennis, Kristin, Natalie, and Heather are there with solid advice for every complicated twist and turn the regulations and markets take; without them, my hair would be many more shades of grey.

To Dr. Daniel Rivetti, my real estate finance professor at the University of San Diego MBA program, and the one who opened my eyes to the world of real estate finance.

To Kirk, Sandra, Greg and Ken and the many financial advisors who trust me with their client's funds. Thank you for taking the time to understand the underlying assets and value in mortgage pools. I appreciate your trust and confidence, and will work diligently to continue to earn it.

To my early investors Marshall, Alan, Norman, and Ken who put their trust in me in the beginning stages of the funds.

To my bankers Darla, Andrea, Tony and Sandra who have helped me throughout the years.

To the California Mortgage Association, a group of private money lenders, of which I am proud to be a member. Thank you to all the members who give of their time and knowledge to educate the members and promote ethics and professionalism in our industry.

To Rosemary and my entire Vistage (formerly TEC) group, thank you for helping me see the forest through trees and holding me accountable to my goals.

To Lisa, Patty, Carol, Liz, Eddie and Steve, and their team at New Century Title Company, who have helped educate, train, and refine our team for many years.

To Darrow, Sandra, Jack, Holly, Martin & Robin and their team of professionals: their belief in our loans and company provide us liquidity to enable us to provide great loans to our borrowers.

To Stacey, Denise, and Marcie for crafting great marketing, graphic design work, and branding so our image is as solid as our returns.

To Keith of Graphix Communications, thank you for a great cover, and your assistance in proofing the layout.

To Marion Wingfield and Ben Williamson, may they both rest in peace, for sharing their daily humor and wisdom as auctioneers on the courthouse steps.

To my mother, for always being there and encouraging me to pursue what made me happy. And to my father, for showing me the spirit and drive of an entrepreneur, and for believing in my capabilities early in my business career.

To all my friends and family who have always supported me. A special thank you Dan and Brad who have tirelessly responded to investor requests for references.

To Robert for convincing me to expand my horizons and develop the first mortgage pool.

To Susan for her love and unwavering support of all my pursuits, and for her expertise in helping me simplify complicated concepts.

Each day I think about my two wonderful children—Daniel, six, and Jordan, nine—who remind me on a regular basis, "If you're the boss, why do you have to work?" One day they will understand that by earning higher yields, I was able to provide for their continuing education and well-being.

Introduction

Most investors want to earn high yields with reduced risk. Mortgage Pools offer an excellent opportunity to diversify your portfolio and increase your investment yield with few asset management headaches.

As a fund manager for two California mortgage pools managing over three hundred investors and hundreds of loans, I have gained insight into what to look for when analyzing a mortgage pool investment.

It always amazes me how little investors really know about the company in which they are investing. I have given dozens of seminars and met with hundreds of investors, and maybe one out of ten asks the smart questions that let him or her make a sound investment decision.

Once the right questions are asked, it is important to verify the information. Mortgage pools are relatively sophisticated investment vehicles, and performing due diligence can be complicated.

I put this book together to unravel the mystery of mortgage pools and their underlying assets. I want investors to intimately understand mortgage pools and how to conduct enough research to determine whether this is the right investment for them.

So how high are "high yields?" Of course it depends on what is happening in the current economic market and the type of fund. To give you a general idea, as of the first quarter of 2006, bank CDs and money markets are offering between 4 and 5 percent annual returns. Most mortgage pools return 9 to 12 percent net yield or more to the investor. You should expect to obtain at least twice the return of the short-term bank lending rate for your extra efforts and the added risk.

Obtaining higher yields takes work. But with thorough due diligence and a comprehensive understanding of the investment, you can achieve the yields you desire—and sleep well at night.

Author Background

I graduated from Miami University (Oxford, OH) with a Marketing degree. During my first twelve years out of college, I was in computer sales and operated a variety of entrepreneurial software ventures.

In 1996 I decided to take a break from the computer and software world and go back to school. I graduated Valedictorian from the University of San Diego in 1996 with a Masters of Business Administration (MBA), with an emphasis in real estate and finance. While there, my real estate professor suggested that MBAs should obtain a real estate broker license, because it gives a new MBA graduate many more opportunities for success.

He wasn't kidding. At the time, real estate broker students were required to complete one of ten projects at the end of each course. I chose "Attend a foreclosure auction and write an essay on what you observe." The auction I attended was scheduled one sunny morning at 10:00 on the courthouse steps in San Diego. I had no idea the turn my life was about to take.

I was struck by the primitive nature of the auction. Dozens of homes listed for sale were simply scribbled on pieces of paper and attached to a clipboard. It was hard for me to believe that people would just let their homes go in this manner. But what intrigued me even more was the shroud of mystery and secrecy around the auction. How did auction bidders find out about these properties? How did they know what loans were on title? How did they value properties they couldn't get inside to inspect? Bidders at the auction shared nothing, and there were no published books at the time about how to buy houses at auction.

For the next several months, I became a student of the foreclosure process. I went to the auctions daily and started reverse engineering the entire auction process. Each time someone bought a property; I would drive by the property, analyze the title records and property value, and figure out what it was about that property that the bidder wanted.

I bought my first property in August 1997. I was the only bidder and paid a penny over the auction's opening bid. Within a few months, I remodeled the home, resold it, and made a nice profit. That same year I bought five more homes, and the next year twenty-five homes, then one hundred or more homes each year thereafter. Over an eight-year period, I bought over five hundred homes and learned a tremendous amount about how to value and appraise residential property, quickly analyze property titles, and understand the psyche of a home-owner in foreclosure. I had no idea how valuable this background would be later in my career as a loan underwriter and originator.

In 2002, I stopped buying properties at foreclosure auctions. Homeowners with equity should never lose their homes in foreclosure. I tired of seeing them evicted with nowhere to go. Instead, I bought homes directly from homeowners before the foreclosure auction—I was able to give the homeowners a fair price and get them out of a real bind.

These homeowners do not want to sell their homes. They are delinquent on their loans and want someone to help dig them out of their holes so they can get fresh starts. The problem is that there are very few loan programs for these poor-credit borrowers, so they are forced to sell their homes or risk losing them at foreclosure auctions.

I experimented with loan programs for delinquent borrowers and successfully created a formula that simultaneously benefits the homeowner, the investor pro-viding the funds, and the loan officer processing the loan. At first I loaned my own money. Once successful, I pooled money from investors and created my first mortgage pool. I saw the clear benefits of sub-prime lending, eventually stopped buying real estate, and focused solely on sub-prime residential lending.

Although I started my business at the foreclosure auctions, ironically, only about 25 percent of the loans I originate are from borrowers in foreclosure. Most are from carefully selected borrowers who have low credit scores for a variety of rea-sons and do not qualify for other loan programs.

Since I started pooling funds, I have only had to foreclose on three properties out of more than 1,500 loans originated. I'm proud of that record. My focus is to help homeowners and give them fresh starts, not to take their homes. As a lender, if I have to foreclose on a property, I view it as a personal failure. I try hard to work with borrowers to find solutions to their financial predicaments and try hard not to create new problems.

Loans are the underlying assets of mortgage pools. Underwriting loans properly is the key to operating a successful mortgage pool. Understanding how loans are underwritten is the key to analyzing the risk of mortgage pool investments and the key to minimizing that risk.

Think of a mortgage pool as you would a house. The foundation of the house is the borrower's ability to repay the loan, the ground floor is the equity in the home, the second story of the house consists of the individual loans that collateralize the pool, and the roof is the mortgage pool in which you are buying shares.

This book will help you ask the right questions in order to understand how the mortgage pool 'house' in which you are investing in is constructed.

What You Will Learn from This Book

- The ABCs of investing in a mortgage pool: what mortgage pools are, how they are structured, and the types of security offerings available
- How to compare and contrast offering memoranda from different mortgage pools
- Questions about mortgage pools you can ask your financial advisor, accountant, and attorney
- The different types of mortgage pools and how to conduct due diligence
- Industry terms used in underwriting, lending, and mortgage pool management
- The inner workings of the sub-prime mortgage market and the nature of poor-credit borrowers
- How a mortgage pool recovers nonperforming assets through foreclosure
- The pros and cons of investing in whole notes versus investing in mortgage pools

Things You Are Not Going to Get from This Book

- Individual financial advice. Every investor's financial picture is unique. This book should primarily be used to create discussion points between you and your trusted financial and legal advisors.

- The ins and outs of investing in whole-loan mortgages. You will learn about the industry along with some basic terminology, but do not expect to be able to underwrite a loan or buy an existing loan after reading this book.

- The intricacy of the law as it pertains to loans and lending. There are many complex federal and state laws governing mortgage pools and sub-prime lending. Some of the legal analysis will be presented to point out various characteristics of loans and mortgage pools, but there are many more laws that will not be discussed. Consult an attorney or a financial advisor before making loans or investments in loans.

- How to earn high yields by trading stocks and bonds. This book is specifically tailored to understand California mortgage pools and their underlying assets.

- How to buy foreclosures. Although foreclosures in California are reviewed as a means of recovering assets from nonperforming loans, this book will not cover the ins and outs of buying foreclosure property. Foreclosure laws vary by state and should be carefully reviewed by your attorney.

Mortgage Pool Basics

A mortgage pool is a generic term for a financial entity in which the underlying assets are mortgages. Think of a mortgage pool as a mutual fund, but instead of stocks or bonds in the mutual fund, the fund holds mortgages. There is no legal entity called a mortgage pool, and there is no legal definition that specifies what something must be in order to be referred to as a mortgage pool.

The heart of a mortgage pool consists of the underlying mortgages. When a borrower takes out a mortgage, the loan is comprised of two basic components: a promise to repay the debt and a recorded document that is evidence of the debt.

The promise to repay is usually in the form of a promissory note, or a revolving line of credit agreement, that spells out the terms of the promise. The recorded document (recorded in the county in which the real estate is located) is usually in the form of a mortgage or a trust deed. When the trust deed or mortgage is recorded, the promise to repay the debt is secured to the property and considered a 'lien.' Whether a mortgage or a trust deed is used depends on the state in which the document is recorded. Some states use mortgages and some use trust deeds. The difference between the two is technical and not relevant to the discussion at hand. Throughout this book, the terms *trust deed, mortgage,* and *loan* will be used interchangeably (See Lending Terms and Concepts).

Mortgage Pool Names

Mortgage pools are often referred to under several different colloquial names, such as Residential Mortgage Backed Securities (RMBS), Asset-Backed Securities (ABS), mortgage REITS, limited partnerships, offering memorandums, and "Reg D" offerings.

Before investing in a mortgage pool, it is critical to understand the exact nature and legal composition of the mortgage pool. Understanding the composition of the pool will give you the basis to conduct due diligence and ask important questions about the pool and the management of the pool in which you are investing.

Mortgages and hence mortgage pools, are securities. Most people think of a security as a stock or bond they sell through a stockbroker or online trading site. The actual definition of a security is much broader, however.

The 1933 Securities Act defines a "security" as "any note, stock, treasury stock, security future, bond, debenture, *evidence of indebtedness…*" (emphasis added).

A mortgage is "evidence of indebtedness" and hence a security.

Securities are generally regulated by the Securities and Exchange Commission (SEC). Some exemptions include:

- Private offerings to a limited number of persons
- Offerings of limited size
- Intrastate offerings

By exempting small offerings from the registration process, the SEC seeks to foster capital formation by lowering the cost of offering securities to the public.[1]

Mortgage Pools vs. Other Types of Pools

Every mortgage pool is unique and must be carefully reviewed. That an investment is referred to as mortgage pool does not mean it conforms to any established standard, that it is "guaranteed" in any way (unless specified in the offering), or that it is endorsed by the governing agency. Because there are no standards, it is critical that you *carefully read* the offering memorandum provided with the investment presented to you. Be sure that you understand the individual characteristics of the entity in which you are investing. This book will give you insights into what to look for so you can ask the management of the mortgage pool meaningful questions.

Two types of funds that are not mortgage pools but have similar characteristics are (1) funds that own real estate and (2) collateralized mortgage obligations.

---

1. From the SEC website—Laws that govern securities: *http://www.sec.gov/about/laws.shtml.*

Funds That Own Real Estate

Real estate funds "pool" money, but they should not be confused with mortgage pools. Real estate funds own real estate, whereas mortgage pools lend money secured by real estate. There are many types of real estate partnerships that own property. For example, some funds buy and develop vacant land, some may develop commercial property, or some may own office buildings, and collect rents from tenants. Growth occurs through appreciation on the underlying real estate owned by the fund. There is typically less regular cash distributions paid but there is substantially more upside for future appreciation.

Collateralized Mortgage Obligation (CMO)

CMOs are similar to mortgage pools but are not structured in quite the same way. Investors in a CMO are not shareholders but rather lenders to an entity. That entity owns the underlying mortgages.

One 'pool' is not necessarily better than another, but the bottom line is that there are many different types of entities. You need to know exactly what you are investing in, and how that investment meets with your financial objectives.

Types of Mortgage Pool Offerings

Offerings of mortgage pool securities take many shapes and forms. Offerings are regulated either by the SEC or the securities division of a particular state. Offerings under SEC regulations are either "Reg D" offerings or "fully registered" offerings. State-regulated offerings are exempt from SEC requirements.

SEC "Reg D" Offering

This offering is a limited offer and sale of securities as governed by Regulation D of the Securities Act of 1933 and usually called a "Reg D" offering. An excellent index of Reg D is provided by the University of Cincinnati College of Law's Securities Lawyer's Deskbook at http://www.law.uc.edu/CCL/33ActRls/regD.html.

Many detailed regulations apply to Reg D offerings, but following are descriptions of the two most important rules for individual investors to be aware of:

Advertising

The Reg D offering may not be advertised. The basic premise of a Reg D offering is that it is limited to "known parties." Unless the offering is fully registered with the SEC, the parties offering the security may not advertise to the general public, conduct seminars, etc. The exact language from the SEC is:

Except as provided in Rule 504(b)(1), neither the issuer nor any person acting on its behalf shall offer or sell the securities by any form of general solicitation or general advertising, including, but not limited to, the following:

    a.   Any advertisement, article, notice or other communication published in any newspaper, magazine, or similar media or broadcast over television or radio; and

    b.   Any seminar or meeting whose attendees have been invited by any general solicitation or general advertising.

Accredited Investors

Unlike a public registered security (like a stock or bond), only persons of a certain financial stature (considered accredited) may invest. The rationale of the SEC is that because the security is of a limited nature and is not publicly traded, only more sophisticated investors should invest. Specific accredited-investor rules that apply to individual investors are:

a. Any natural person whose individual net worth, or joint net worth with that person's spouse, at the time of his purchase exceeds $1,000,000;

b. Any natural person who had an individual income in excess of $200,000 in each of the two most recent years or joint income with that person's spouse in excess of $300,000 in each of those years and has a reasonable expectation of reaching the same income level in the current year;

c. Any trust, with total assets in excess of $5,000,000, not formed for the specific purpose of acquiring the securities offered, whose purchase is directed by a sophisticated person as described in Rule 506(b)(2)(ii).

SEC Fully Registered Offering

A fully registered offering is one which is in compliance with the 1933 and 1934 Securities and Exchange Acts. Companies meeting this standard are under a higher level of scrutiny by the SEC and report regularly to the SEC. Fully registered companies must submit comprehensive quarterly and annual reports to the SEC, which are then made available to the general public.

A company fully registered with the SEC is a "public company," but it may or may not be listed on a stock exchange. Whether to list on a stock exchange is a choice up to each company registered with the SEC. Just because a company is fully registered, however, does not guarantee the performance of the fund.

If a pool is not listed on an exchange, it must register in accordance with each state's "blue sky law" and conform to that state's individual security offering requirements with regard to the type of investors the pool may accept and the type of advertising it may do.

The term "blue sky" most likely comes from an opinion of Justice McKenna of the United States Supreme Court in 1917. Justice McKenna wrote the Court's opinion in *Hall vs. Geiger-Jones Co.*, 242 U.S. 539 (1917), dealing with the constitutionality of state securities regulations. Justice McKenna described investments that were speculative as having "…so many feet of blue sky."[1]

State-Regulated Offerings (SEC-Exempt)

A company that offers securities only in the state in which it is chartered is exempt from filing with the Securities and Exchange Commission, as provided for by rule 3a of the Securities Act of 1933.

California Requirements

In California, the Department of Corporations Securities Regulation Division (http://www.corp.ca.gov/srd/security.htm) governs securities offered in the state.

California must be the investors' state of primary residence at the time of investing. In addition, the company offering the security must conduct 80 percent of its business within the state of California. If either of these two provisions is violated, the company must register the offering with the SEC as either a limited or a fully registered offering.

State-regulated offerings in California differ from Reg D limited offerings in two significant ways:

Advertising

The company is permitted to advertise to the general public, provided such advertising is approved by the Department of Corporations.

Investor Suitability Standards

The threshold for what the SEC calls an "accredited investor" is different for state offerings. In California, each company submitting for a securities permit from the Department of Corporations is subject to individual approval based on the terms and conditions of the offering. The investor-suitability standard is often considerably lower than that required for an SEC-type offering.

---

1.   Quoted on seclaw.com.

Licensing: DOC vs. DRE

In addition to requiring a permit or registration to offer the security for sale to the general public, the entity purchasing or originating loans may also require a license.

If the entity you are reviewing for investment does not have the proper licensing, do not invest. In California, for non-banking activities, two entities issue licenses to originate mortgages: the Department of Corporations (DOC) and the California Department of Real Estate (DRE).

Department of Corporations (DOC)

The Department of Corporations (DOC) issues two origination licenses: a California Finance Lender license (CFL) and a Residential Mortgage Lender (RML) license.

California Finance Lender License (CFL)

The DOC issues a CFL license to companies that give them lending authority.

A *finance lender* is defined in the law as "any person who is engaged in the business of making consumer loans or making commercial loans." A finance lender license provides the licensee with an exemption from the usury provision of the California Constitution.

Employees of a CFL may originate loans with consumers, with other DRE brokers, or with other CFL lenders. CFL lenders are subjected to annual reporting of information, but loan officers who are employees of the CFL do not have to take a licensing exam.

Residential Mortgage Lender (RML)

An RML is granted under the California Residential Mortgage Lender Act. This Act was specifically enacted to regulate activities of mortgage bankers. (See the Mortgage Brokers vs. Mortgage Bankers section.)

Although there are several nuances with the two licenses, basically a CFL is a license to work with consumers and other CFLs, and a RML is a license to work with institutions.

There is little difference between the two for an investor to be concerned about, and for investment purposes one license is not necessarily better than the other.

Guarantee

The Department of Corporations allows some companies to offer a guaranteed class of shares. The term *guaranteed* can be misleading. The guarantee is a partial guarantee and is typically $1 set aside for every $8 invested.

If, for example, a fund wanted to issue $10 million worth of "guaranteed" Class A shares, the fund would have to show a net worth of $10 million x 12.5 percent ($1 for every $8 invested) = $1,250,000. To qualify from the DOC to offer the guaranteed class of shares, the mortgage pool submits an audited financial statement showing the net worth.

Guaranteed shares are usually offered at a substantially lower rate than non-guaranteed shares, sometimes the yield spread may be as great as 3 to 5 percent.

Personally, I do not care for a guaranteed class of stock for investors as it pertains to California DOC mortgage pools, for three reasons:

1. The guarantee is really for only 12.5 percent of your investment, which, frankly, isn't that substantial.

2. The guarantee is only a guarantee from the manager of the fund, which is usually not that substantial an entity. By that, I mean that the fund manager typically is not rated by a Fitch, Mood's, or S & P, and it's not a chartered bank. Many investors somehow assume that a guarantee means there's usually some type of federal or state guarantee implied. There is not.

3. Demonstrating a net worth equal to 12.5 percent of the invested guaranteed class of stock is not the same as having cash set aside. Net worth could be equity in an office building or other equity that may or may not be liquid if the guarantee is required due to a fund failure.

Bottom line: for the significant reduction in yield, the guarantee does not get you much in terms of protecting your assets.

Department of Real Estate (DRE)

The DRE licenses individuals and corporations to originate and broker loans. Licensees must pass an exam and hang their licenses with a broker. They also are subject to continuing-education requirements. A broker is subject to higher-education and exam standards. However, most of the education and exam standards relate to buying and selling real estate and not to underwriting and originating loans.

A DRE licensee is not required to apply for a CFL license, but he or she may elect to also obtain a CFL license.

Which License is Better…DOC or DRE?

At first glance, it would appear that a Department of Real Estate (DRE) license is better. After all, a licensed real estate agent required to take an exam and submit to a regular educational requirement would of course be preferred to just an employee of a California Finance Lender as required by the Department of Corporations (DOC). But things are not always as they seem. The DRE agent's license is mostly designed for buying and selling property, and the coursework and requirements are not well tailored to a licensee who plans to broker consumer loans.

The type of license is not as important to investment success as are the underwriting guidelines, staff, training, company experience, and individual product knowledge.

What's important from an investor's perspective is that the company has a license and is properly operating under the guidelines established by the regulatory agency.

Terms and Concepts—Mortgage Pools

There are many terms used in the mortgage pool and sub-prime lending world. Understanding how the industry operates and the terms it uses will help you understand the company and the mortgage investments of the mortgage pool.

Offering Memorandum

The offering memorandum (offering) is the way the mortgage pool operates. It describes everything from the types of loans accepted into the pool, the ways that earnings are distributed, and the risks associated with the pool. Offering memoranda always include operating agreements or corporate bylaws. **Always read the complete offering memorandum.** (See Offering Memorandum section for more details.)

Operating Agreement or Corporate Bylaws

An operating agreement is an agreement among the company's members that governs the company's operations and the rights of its members. Operating agreements apply primarily to a Limited Liability Company (LLC) or a Limited Liability Partnership (LLP). Corporations use a similar document often called 'corporate bylaws.'

The operating agreement will control important items such as how the members vote on dissolving the company, electing a new manager, or making changes to the way the company operates.

Subscription Agreement

A subscription agreement is the document that you complete in order to make the investment. You are subscribing with the company for a certain number of shares. It provides the company information about the name in which you want the shares vested, and confirms that you are qualified to invest.

Due Diligence

Due Diligence means "the care that a prudent person might be expected to exercise in the examination and evaluation of risks affecting a business transaction."[1] It is the research you conduct to verify that the company is what it purports to be. (See the Due Diligence section for a detailed discussion of topics to research.)

Types of Loans

Loans are generally structured as *closed ended* or *opened ended*.

Closed ended—a loan in which the amount borrowed is finite. For example, a borrower purchases a home and receives a $250,000 loan. The loan is said to be closed, because the borrower may not receive more than $250,000.

Open ended—a loan in which the amount borrowed may change over time. These loans are often referred to as a "revolving line of credit" or "home equity line of credit" (HELOC). The borrower is approved for a maximum credit line and may draw from the line up to the approved amount. Interest is only charged on the funds used. If for example, a borrower draws down $50,000, interest is charged the day the funds are borrowed. If the borrower pays down principal of $30,000 the next month, interest is then charged on the remaining $20,000 and the monthly payment is adjusted to a lower amount based on the new outstanding balance.

Types of Properties

Mortgage Pools consist of loans secured by real estate. Some funds specialize in one type of real estate, and other funds may have a mix of real estate.

Residential

Residential property is typically single-family homes, duplexes (two units attached), condos, planned urban developments (PUDs), town homes, co-ops, manufactured homes, triplexes (three units), and fourplexes (four units). The foregoing types of residential property are often referred to collectively as "1-4 Units."

---

1.   Definition from dictionary.com.

Land

Land is raw land, improved or unimproved. Improved land typically has utilities and possibly roads already established, whereas unimproved land does not.

Commercial

Commercial property includes property not otherwise included in the Residential or Land categories such as shopping centers, apartment buildings, office buildings, industrial complexes, etc.

Terms and Concepts—Lending

The following terms and concepts are frequently used by lenders to describe and discuss various attributes of loans:

Trust Deed/Mortgage

Trust deeds and mortgages can be thought of as synonymous. Both documents are evidence of the debt. The documents are typically recorded in the county in which the property is located in order to put the world on notice that the owner of the trust deed has a lien on that particular property.

Some states are set up as "trust deed" states and others as "mortgage" states. In trust deed states, a trustee is assigned as a neutral third party between the beneficiary (lender) and the trustor (borrower). The trustee is said to hold "naked title" to the property, and when the debt is repaid, the trustee reconveys the note on behalf of the beneficiary. Mortgage states operate as two-party systems between lender and borrower with no trustee needed.

Loan to Value (LTV)

LTV is the ratio of the loan amount to the value of the property. LTV is a key determinant used by lenders to qualify borrowers for a loan program and to determine the interest rate. For example, if a borrower was applying for a $300,000 first mortgage, and the appraised value of the home was $400,000, the LTV would be $300,000/$400,000 or 75 percent.

Second Position (A.K.A. Junior Position)

Loans on title are ranked according to seniority of title. The ranking determines which lender gets paid from proceeds in the event of a foreclosure. A typical loan used to buy or refinance a home is in first, or senior, position: it is the senior-most secured position on title and is first in line to receive proceeds from a foreclosure auction in the event that a property is foreclosed upon.

A loan secured by the property that does not pay off the first loan is said to be in "second position." Equity lines of credit are typically (but not always) in second position. Second-position loans are more risky than first-position loans, because if the first loan is not paid, the lender may foreclose. Laws vary by state. In some states, like California, the second mortgage holder may reinstate the first mortgage and begin a foreclosure of their own. In other states, like Connecticut, the second must pay off the first in order to foreclose. In either case, the second-position lender must have enough liquidity to advance to the first mortgage holder. Advancing to prevent a foreclosure is referred to as "protecting your position."

Combined Loan to Value (CLTV)

CLTV is the ratio of the combined loan amount to the value of the property. It is used to determine a borrower's qualification to receive a junior-position loan and the interest rate to be paid. For example, assume a borrower with an existing first mortgage of $250,000 applies for a second-position mortgage of $50,000, and the value of the home is $400,000. The CLTV is the sum of the existing first lien plus the new junior-position lien divided by the value of the home: ($250,000 + $50,000)/$400,000 = 75 percent CLTV.

Originating Loans

Loan origination is the process of creating the loan. The entity creating the documentation for the loan (promissory note, trust deed, disclosures, etc.) is said to be the "originator" of the loan.

Purchasing Loans

Many mortgage pools purchase loans that have been originated by another company. Purchasing loans does not generally require a license. However, if the entity is purchasing loans shortly after the loans are originated, the entity may be required to have a license. Consider these two examples:

1. If ABC company purchases ten loans that were originated six months ago from XYZ company, no license is required.

2. If ABC company purchased the ten loans one day after XYZ company originated them, then ABC company may be considered an "originator" and will most likely be required to have a license in order to purchase the loans. Laws vary by state with regard to when a company may be

considered a loan originator. When conducting due diligence on a company purchasing loans, it is important to ask about the loan-purchasing procedures and inquire whether or not a license is required.

FICO Scores and Credit grades

Today's mortgage lending industry is dominated by a function of the borrower's credit score as determined by Fair Isaac Corporation (FICO).

The credit score takes into account numerous factors, including types of credit, payment history, duration of credit, length of credit, maximum credit lines, and other credit-related factors.

Although each lender sets its own credit-score-determining factors, the industry follows these general guidelines:

Category	FICO Score
Prime:	700 and above
Alt-A:	670 to 700
Alt-B:	620 to 670
Sub-prime:	620 and under

Source: National Mortgage News Research/2006 MID (Eleventh Edition)

The lower the FICO score, the worse the credit. Most mortgage pools obtain high yields for their investors by focusing on the sub-prime category of borrowers.

ABCs (and Ds) of Credit Grading

In addition to the FICO credit score, lenders also categorize borrowers with letters representing a credit grade. Credit grades are based on several factors: the number of times the borrower was late on his or her mortgage (called lates) whether there was a bankruptcy (BK) and how long ago it was, and whether there has been a foreclosure action (NOD, for Notice of Default)[1] and how long ago it

---

1. NOD is a recorded Notice of Default in a non-judicial foreclosure used in trust-deed states such as California. Many states use different methods to determine when and how a loan goes into foreclosure, the details of which are not discussed in this book and are not relevant to this discussion.

was. Mortgage lates are typically represented by the number of lates in a give period (thirty, sixty, or ninety days). For example, 0x30 means no mortgage lates, 1x30 means one mortgage payment was thirty to fifty-nine days late, 2x60 means two mortgage payments were sixty to eighty-nine days late, etc.

A typical grouping of credit grades is as follows:

Credit Grade	Description
AA	0x30, No BK last 24 mo., No NOD last 36 mo.
A	1x30, No BK last 24 mo., No NOD last 24 mo.
A-	4x30, No BK last 24 mo., No NOD last 24 mo.
B	2x60, No BK last 18 mo., No NOD last 12 mo.
C	3x60 & 1x90, No BK last 18 mo., No NOD last 12 mo.

The three credit bureaus—Equifax, TransUnion, and Experian—launched a new credit scoring system called "VantageScore" to compete with the FICO method. As of March 2006, this system was not in use, although it may be used in the future. Using VantageScore, consumers are graded between 500 and 990 as follows:

VantageScore

Category	VantageScore
A	901-990
B	801-900
C	701-800
D	601-700
F	501-600

Source: Associated Press, Eileeen Alt Powell, 6:33 AM, 3/14/06

The B and C credit grade segments of the sub-prime market have experienced the most rapid growth.

Year	Total Res. Production	B & C Volume	B & C% Of Total
2005	$2,800	$580	20.7%
2004	$2,790	$608	21.8%
2003	$3,904	$390	9.9%
2002	$2,787	$241	8.6%
2001	$2,066	$180	8.7%
2000	$1,067	$134	12.5%
1995	$639	$35	5.5%

Notes: Sub-prime loans include credit ratings that are A-to D in quality but also may include other product types including IO mortgages, payment option loans, and even alt-A.

Source: National Mortgage News/MID Quarterly Data Report ($ in billions)

Appraisal

An appraisal is an expert valuation of the real estate completed by a licensed appraiser. There are several appraisal specialties as well. Appraisers may have special training to evaluate land, commercial properties, apartment buildings, etc.

Appraisals are often validated by a Broker Price Opinion and/or an Automated Valuation Model.

Broker Price Opinion (BPO)

BPOs are often obtained by loan originators to confirm appraisal values. The BPO is typically a one- or two-page document, less comprehensive than an appraisal and based on real estate listings in the proximity of the property. It is a broker's assessment of what the property would sell for in the current market conditions.

Automated Valuation Model (AVM)

AVMs are frequently used to confirm values and prevent appraisal fraud. The lender submits the address of the property, and, using public information and sophisticated modeling techniques, the AVM returns the estimated value of the property.

AVMs cannot always account for positive attributes of a property, like view, location on a golf course, or negative aspects such as roof deterioration, etc.

Debt Service

Debt service is the amount of debt the borrower is obligated to pay. This amount is usually expressed in monthly payment terms. For example, if a borrower pays the following:

First Mortgage	$1,500/month
Car Loan	$ 250/month
Credit Cards	$ 300/month
Taxes	$ 125/month
Total	$2,175/month of debt service.

Lenders use monthly debt service to calculate a Debt-to-Income ratio, which is used to qualify or disqualify a borrower for a loan product.

Debt to Income Ratio (DTI)

DTI is the ratio of monthly debt service to monthly income. Lenders use this ratio to determine loan program qualifications and interest rates and to accept or deny borrowers' applications for loan products. Monthly income is the gross amount the borrower earns each month.

Some lenders use a "front-end" ratio, which includes all debt service except the monthly mortgage debt service; others use a "back-end" ratio, which does include the monthly mortgage debt service as well as all other debt.

For example, if Mr. Miller earns $6,000 a month and has the following expenses:

Credit Card Minimum Monthly Payments	$500
Property Taxes	$1,000
Insurance	$150

Auto Payments	$500
Total	$2,150

Mr. Miller's front-end ratio would be $2,150/6,000 = 36 percent. This indicates that Mr. Miller's monthly recurring expenses, not including his mortgage, are 36 percent of his gross monthly income.

If Mr. Miller's mortgage payment was $1,000/month, then his back-end ratio would be $3,150/$6,000 = 53 percent.

The higher the debt-to-income ratio is, the riskier the loan. Most sub-prime lenders have an underwriting guideline that back-end ratios should not exceed 55 percent.

Defined Benefit for Borrower

Loans should be written for the benefit of the borrower. Many states have laws that state that a loan may not be written unless there is a "defined benefit" for the borrower. A defined benefit may be debt consolidation, stopping a foreclosure, obtaining a lower interest rate, reducing payments, etc. Loans should not be written solely for the benefit of the lender.

Income Verification

Income can be verified in several ways, and each lender has different underwriting guidelines for verifying income.

The industry generally has four different types of income-related verifications:

Full Doc (short for full documentation)

Full documentation is provided to the lender to support the income written on the mortgage application. If Mr. Miller indicates that he earns $6,000 a month, he must provide whatever documentation the lender requires to substantiate this income. For example, some lenders will require his W-2 statement; others require a W-2 plus bank statements and tax returns. Income-verification requirements vary widely by lender.

Lite Doc (short for lite documentation)

Lite documentation loans vary widely by lender. Usually they require some documentation, though less than what is required for a full doc loan. For example, say the lender requires twelve months' worth of bank statements to support Mr. Miller's W-2 wage statement, but Mr. Miller started his job only six months ago and can only provide six months' worth of statements. The interest rate and fees may go up slightly to compensate for the lack of full documentation.

Stated Income

The borrower provides no documentation and simply "states" his income on the mortgage application.

At one end of the spectrum, stated income loans are offered to very high credit-score borrowers as a method of making the loan more convenient for the applicant. Mrs. Smith may have a FICO score of 750, and statistically, FICO scores of 750 and above have a very low incident of delinquency or foreclosure. Based on the credit score, the lender will not require any further income documentation.

On the other end of the spectrum are borrowers that have low credit scores but have significant equity in their property. A statement from the borrower may be sufficient to satisfy the underwriting guidelines.

Good lenders evaluate candidates on their ability to repay in addition to the underlying collateral for the loan. Most states do not permit loans solely based upon equity.

Loan Program/Product

The industry refers to "loan programs" or "loan products," and people often are confused about what these terms mean. Think of a portable stereo: there are many options to consider, from what size stereo you want to what optional equipment you want with it (CD player, equalizer, etc.). Just so, loan products and programs also have different features and options available.

Examples of loan features include "interest only" loans, which require a payment of interest only for a period of time. Another feature may be that the loan is tied to a particular index that adjusts more slowly than others. Industry analysts group these features into loan products/programs and use them to describe the loans that they want to invest in or to grade with a particular credit score.

Equity

Equity is the difference between the current market value of the property and the amount owed on the property. For example, if Mr. Miller's home is worth $500,000 and he owes $300,000, then he is said to have $200,000 in equity.

Promissory Note or Revolving Line of Credit Agreement

A promissory note is a written agreement to repay a debt with specific terms at a given date. Equity lines of credit use a document similar to a promissory note called a Revolving Line of Credit Agreement. This agreement also outlines the agreement to repay the debt, but includes specific terms regarding drawing down and repaying the line of credit.

Prepayment Penalty or Early Termination Fee

A Prepayment Penalty or Early Termination Fee is a fee paid by a borrower if the loan is paid off earlier than an agreed-upon date. The amount of the penalty/fee varies depending on the loan product, the state in which the loan was originated, and by whom the loan is arranged. The concept behind a prepayment penalty is that the lender will charge less up front for a loan, but in return for the effort to write the loan, the borrower will agree to pay interest for some minimum period of time. If this minimum is not met, the lender is compensated with a fee.

Prepayment penalty is generally a penalty equal to six months of interest on 80 percent of the loan balance. An early termination fee is a fee to terminate a line of credit and is often substantially less than six months' interest.

Rate Sheet

Lenders publish "rate sheets," which give mortgage brokers/bankers the available interest rates on loan programs based on credit grades, loan amounts, and credit scores. Rate sheets change daily or weekly depending on the lender and/or the loan program.

Secondary Market and Securitization

The secondary market is a term used to refer to the re-sale of loans. Loans can either be held by the lender originating the loan, or sold to a third party. When loans are held by a lender, it is called 'portfolio lending', because the loans are held in the lender's portfolio of assets. Most lenders sell their loans to a third party as a means to obtain liquidity and reduce risk. The process of bundling loans to sell to a third party is called 'securitization.' The securitization is typically in the form a bond that is then traded on Wall Street in a market place referred to as the 'secondary market.' The secondary market for loans is over a trillion dollars.

Mortgage Pools are a form of securitization. Loans originated by pool managers are bundled into an entity, and shares of the entity are sold to investors.

Yield Spread Premium (YSP)

The "yield" refers to the interest rate. "Spread" refers to the difference between the stated interest rate on the rate sheet and the interest rate "sold" to the borrower. The "premium" refers to the amount offered by the lender to the broker and/or mortgage banker for obtaining the spread.

For example, if the interest on the rate sheet for a particular borrower's qualification is 7 percent, and the loan officer "sells" the borrower on 8 percent, then the Yield Spread Premium is 1 percent (the difference between 8 percent "sold" to the borrower and 7 percent on the rate sheet).

The mortgage broker or banker gets a "bonus" for getting the borrower to accept a higher interest rate. An example of a bonus may be 0.5 point for every 1 point additional rate. (A point is a percentage, so 0.5 point equals 0.5 percent).

Weighted Average Cost of Borrowing/Blended Rate

The weighted average cost of borrowing, or blended rate, is used when describing the interplay of two loans: a senior-position first mortgage and a junior-position equity line of credit (HELOC), for example. Many mortgage pools increase their yields by underwriting HELOCs. Investors often wonder why a borrower would pay 14 percent for a HELOC when an 11 percent closed-end mortgage may be available.

The answer lies in the blended rate, and is best illustrated by an example.

Mr. Miller lives in California, owns a home worth $500,000 (on which he still owes $300,000), and has a 6 percent interest rate on his first mortgage. He purchased his home when his credit was good, and he was fortunate to get a low interest rate on his mortgage. Last year, Mr. Miller ran into some hard times and was laid off from his job. As a result, he was delinquent on his mortgage and various other bills, and his FICO credit score dropped below 500.

Mr. Miller is getting back on his feet. He has a new job and can afford his home and his monthly payments. However, he has an IRS lien, some high interest credit-card debt, and is three payments delinquent on his home. Unless Mr. Miller borrows $50,000, he could face foreclosure. He consults a loan officer with ABC Lending, and the loan officer advises Mr. Miller that because of his low credit score, the least expensive first mortgage he qualifies for is 11 percent.

To accomplish his debt consolidation objective, Mr. Miller could obtain a new first mortgage:

Pay off Existing Loan	$300,000
Pay off IRS and Credit Cards	$50,000
Loan Fees	$18,000 (typical for a sub-prime loan)
Total New First Mortgage	$368,000 @ 11 percent

Mr. Miller wondered how much more each year this new debt-consolidation loan would cost him.

New First Loan:	$368,000 @ 11 percent = $40,480 interest/year
Existing Loan:	$300,000 @ 6 percent = $18,000 interest/year
Difference:	**$22,480 interest/year**

Mr. Miller thought the excess interest cost sounded high. In fact, he is paying $22,480/$50,000 = **45 percent effective interest rate**. Fortunately, Mr. Miller decided to seek out alternatives.

Another loan officer introduced Mr. Miller to XYZ Lenders, who offer a unique sub-prime, open-ended equity line of credit.

The loan officer told Mr. Miller that instead of refinancing his first mortgage and losing his low interest rate of 6 percent, he could borrow $50,000 using an open-ended line of credit.

First, Mr. Miller looked at the total annual interest he would pay when he combined his existing first mortgage and the new open-ended line of credit:

Existing $300,000 First Loan @ 6 percent	$18,000 interest/year
New $50,000 Open-Ended Loan @ 14 percent	$ 7,000 interest/year
Total Annual Interest	**$25,000 interest/year**

He then compared the total interest on the open-ended line of credit to the total interest he would pay if he refinanced his existing 1st mortgage:

	Annual Interest
Refinancing Entire First Mortgage	$40,480
Keeping First and Adding Open-Ended Line	$25,000
Savings Using the Open-Ended Line	**$15,480 interest/year**

Mr. Miller could see that he was substantially better off choosing the open-ended line of credit, because it allowed him to keep his low interest-rate loan in place on the majority of his debt. Even though the interest rate is higher on the open-ended credit line, the weighted average cost of borrowing and his total interest each year are substantially lower.

The Players

So what's to know? A borrower applies for a loan, he talks to a loan officer, paperwork is exchanged, and voila—a loan is originated.

But who is the loan officer? Who does he work for? Is he licensed—why or why not? Where does the loan officer obtain the funds to originate the loan?

Understanding the players in the industry is critical to understanding how the industry operates and how and why different licenses are required and used.

The Loan Officer

A Loan Officer is the person working directly with the borrower.

Loan officer sounds so official, doesn't it? The word *officer* sounds important—as if the person holding this title is specially trained and educated to "officiate" a transaction.

Loan officers often have no training or education to process, select, or otherwise transact a loan. State lending laws about loan officers differ greatly. Some states require all persons transacting loans to be specially educated and licensed by state-sanctioned programs, but many states do not have specific education requirements.

In any industry there are great loan officers and lousy loan officers. There are great companies that train and educate their loan-officer employees or contractors, and there are lousy ones.

In California, there are two basic types of loan officers: (1) licensed real estate agents and (2) employees of a California Finance Lender (CFL)[1]. Neither option guarantees you are working with an educated and trained loan officer. Real estate

---

1.   There are also RMLs as previously defined, but the loan officer requirements are the same as a CFL and are therefore not separately identified.

agents are primarily trained in buying and selling property, and the license requires virtually no practical lending training.

An employee of a CFL requires no training or licensing whatsoever. The loan officer must simply be a bona fide employee of the CFL.

The lack of uniform qualifications and/or licensing requirements for loan officers is why it is critical to understand the "third-party origination quality control policies" of the manager of the mortgage pool.

Mortgage Brokers vs. Mortgage Bankers

A loan officer has to work for someone. In most cases, the loan officer works for either a mortgage broker or a mortgage banker; sometimes he may be an employee of a bank, savings & loan, or other lending institution. Since most loan officers originating loans for mortgage pools work for mortgage brokers or bankers, that will be the focus of this section.

A mortgage broker is simply a middle-person. The broker (via the loan officer) reviews a borrower's qualifications and finds the best lending program to meet the borrower's needs. Brokers do not have access to all lending programs. Typically, a mortgage broker signs agreements with a few dozen or so lenders that have a variety of loan programs. Think of the mortgage broker as a retail electronics store. Each retail store carries only the brands they choose to display in the store.

Mortgage bankers operate in a similar way to mortgage brokers. The borrower's qualifications are reviewed, and the loan officer working for the mortgage banker selects the best lending program to meet the borrower's needs. The difference is that the lending program offered by the mortgage banker is provided from the mortgage banker's own funds and not from a brokered arrangement with another lender.

Making sure that mortgage brokers and bankers are properly licensed is critical to ensuring the quality of the underlying loans in the mortgage pool. Mortgage pools should have strict quality-control, audit, and fraud-detection mechanisms in place to guard against rogue mortgage brokers and bankers that may employ undereducated and unscrupulous loan officers.

Loan Processing
The Ins and Outs

Loan processing is an art. The end result of a properly processed loan is a comprehensive loan credit file that contains all the supporting documents required by the loan program selected for the borrower and the documentation to show the loan is in compliance with state and federal laws.

Processing a loan is the method of gathering documentation from the borrower to match the borrower's qualification of the loan with the lender's underwriting standards.

It is not always obvious, but sub-prime loans are substantially more difficult to process than prime loans. Sub-prime borrowers often have unique credit and processing challenges that can delay the loan process and require more time be spent to create a proper credit file.

The following section describes loan processing functions (e.g. loan application, payoffs, income, insurance, etc.) and highlights the differences between processing a "prime loan" (credit grade A, A-, or B) and a sub-prime loan (credit grades C, C-, or D).

Loan Application

A loan application is submitted for review to an underwriter. It will typically include a mortgage application (referred to as a '1003' because of the form number at the bottom), which summarizes the borrower's qualifications.

Prime

Loan application is usually pristine, every blank completed, every account identified with addresses and account numbers, and the application is signed and initialed in the right places.

C/D

Loan application often arrives incomplete. In many instances the borrower's credit is in such disarray that he does not know what exactly he owes or to whom he owes it.

Some of the completeness of the application relates to the skills of the loan officer, but many times the loan officer is precluded from submitting a complete application because the borrower does not have the information.

Payoffs

In order for a lender to fund a loan, the lender has to know the ending balance of each account it will pay off.

Prime

Borrower is typically not delinquent and has all the statements showing current balances.

C/D

Borrower often does not have a copy of his most recent account statement, and because the account is typically delinquent, the ending balances are more difficult to obtain (as the lender or escrow agent has to call several parties many times to gather all the necessary costs and fees to pay off the loan).

In addition, this borrower usually has *more* accounts being paid to consolidate debt, and each one is delinquent or the account has been ignored for years.

Sometimes creditors of sub-prime borrowers are not cooperative and will take an extended period of time to gather the amount owed on the delinquent account. Different states have different laws regarding the amount of time a creditor may take to provide a payoff quote. In California, for example, the creditor has twenty-one days to provide a payoff statement.

Often times, when the lender finally does receive the payoff, the number is substantially more than the borrower anticipated, and in many cases could disqualify him from the loan program to which he applied. When this happens, the loan officer may have to re-submit the loan to a different company, or re-submit it to the same company asking for a different loan amount to be considered.

When the lender does receive a complete list of loans to payoff, the payoff expiration dates expire at various times. Imagine five delinquent accounts for which payoffs are obtained, and each payoff is good through a different date. One payoff may be good for four days, one for ten days, etc. Each time a payoff quote expires, the lender or escrow officer has to get an updated one. For a non-delinquent account, the lender can simply add a per diem fee to account for excess interest. This does not work for delinquent accounts, because there are often late charges and attorney fees being added to the account simultaneously with the processing of the loan.

Obtaining payoffs for sub-prime borrowers is often the most time consuming and difficult part of the process and is a substantial part of the additional fees and processing time charged to these borrowers.

Income

Different lenders require different forms of income verification, ranging from W-2 wage forms to bank accounts or tax returns.

Prime

Provides the lender information that supports the income provided on the mortgage application.

C/D

Information provided often does not match what is claimed on the mortgage application, or if it docs match, the information provided is incomplete. In either case, the lender/escrow agent must work with the borrower to obtain the correct documentation for the loan, which delays the loan and increases processing time.

Insurance certificate

Lenders require a new insurance certificate naming the lender on the policy in the event of loss.

Prime

Insurance certificate arrives promptly as needed.

C/D

Borrower is often delinquent with the insurer and the insurer must be paid prior to issuing the certificate. Insured amounts are often inadequate to cover the loan amount, and the lender/escrow agent must obtain a correct certificate.

Lender Disclosures

Lender disclosures are documents sent to the borrower within three days of the date that the loan application is requested, to be signed and returned to continue the loan process. These documents typically include a "statement of information." The title company uses this document to investigate liens and judgments on record. Most title companies will not fund a loan without having this statement completed and signed by the borrower well in advance of the loan funding. It often takes several days after receipt of this document for title companies to complete their search and return the findings to the lender/escrow agent.

Prime

Disclosures and statement of information come back promptly and are complete.

C/D

Documents are often not received back. When documents are received, they are incomplete or unsigned, which delays the process. The most damaging delay for these borrowers is that the title company cannot begin the search for liens and judgments without a completed statement of information. Many times the title company finds liens and judgments that either the borrower didn't know about, forgot, or was trying to conceal from the lender. Once discovered, payoffs and judgments have to be obtained on these liens, which can take several weeks. In the meantime, other payoffs and judgments previously disclosed to the lender have already been obtained and now will have to be updated because the previous payoff date expired. Once the payoff of a newly discovered lien/judgment is obtained, the new lien or judgment amount could disqualify the borrower from the loan program for which he applied, and the process then has to be re-started.

Appraisals

Appraisals are obtained by licensed professionals to independently assess value for the lender.

Prime

Quickly obtains appraisal, which is paid for in advance.

C/D

Borrower typically waits until he knows if he is going to be approved by the lender. Often, the lender is given a value that is just the "belief" by the loan officer and/or borrower. The borrower delays getting the appraisal because he often does not have the funds to advance to the appraiser. The delay in obtaining the appraisal could delay the loan and cause already received pay-offs to expire.

As described, the process of creating a loan file is a detail-oriented task. Processing credit files for sub-prime borrowers is significantly more challenging than processing a credit file for a prime borrower.

Having well-written underwriting guidelines and an experienced management team significantly reduces the risk of underwriting sub-prime loans for the mortgage pool.

Foreclosure
Recovering the Asset

Investors in a mortgage pool want to understand what happens if a loan does not perform. Foreclosure laws vary by state. The following describes the process in California as an example of how a mortgage pool can recover funds from a non-performing loan.

Foreclosure is the process by which a lender recovers nonperforming loans.

Types of Foreclosure

There are two types of foreclosure: judicial foreclosures, which are conducted using the court system, and non-judicial foreclosures, which are conducted without going to court. In California, the vast majority of foreclosures are non-judicial. Because courts do not oversee the process, the California Civil Code (CC Section 2924 et. seq.) provides strict procedures that must be followed before a borrower's home can be foreclosed.

In California, the "deed of trust" is the document that pledges a borrower's property as security for the loan. If the borrower falls behind on his or her payments, the deed of trust gives the lender the right to sell the property at a public auction to pay off the loan.

In a state which uses trust deeds, there are three parties involved: the trustor (the borrower), the beneficiary (the lender), and the trustee (the person or company authorized to foreclose if the borrower defaults on the loan).

The Foreclosure Process

The lender initiates the foreclosure process by requesting that the trustee file a Notice of Default. The non-judicial foreclosure process in California takes a minimum of 111 days from the time the Notice of Default is initially recorded until the property can be sold at a trustee sale.

Timeline

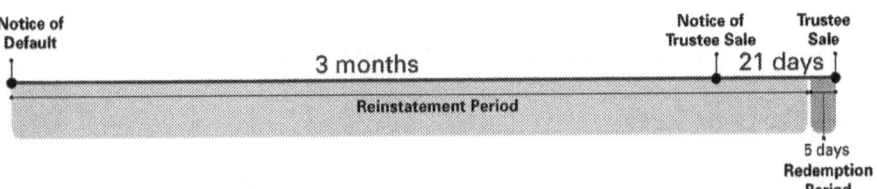

Notice of Default

The Notice of Default is the official document notifying the borrower that the lender has started the foreclosure process to sell the property in order to pay off the loan. The Notice of Default must be filed with the county recorder's office.

Reinstatement Period

The reinstatement period is the time during which the borrower may stop the foreclosure process by bringing your loan current. The reinstatement period begins as soon as the Notice of Default is filed and ends five business days prior to the foreclosure sale.

Notice of Trustee Sale

If the loan is not brought current within three months, a Notice of Trustee Sale is recorded. The Notice of Trustee Sale gives the date, time, and location of the sale of the property. The sale must be at least twenty calendar days after the Notice of Trustee Sale is recorded and is typically between twenty-one and twenty-five days later.

Redemption Period

The redemption period is the last five business days before the trustee sale. During the redemption period, the borrower no longer has the right to reinstate the loan but may redeem the property by paying off the entire unpaid balance plus late fees, penalties, attorney fees, and trustee's costs.

Trustee Sale

The last step in the foreclosure process is the actual public sale of the property. The sale must be conducted on a weekday during normal business hours and usually takes place in front of the county courthouse or another outside location.

Third Party or REO

The amount of the bid at the auction is set by the lender. Provided there is enough equity to secure the lender's lien, the lender typically sets the bid at the total amount owed, including accrued interest, advances to other lenders, attorney fees, trustee fees, and any other fees required to foreclose. If there is not enough equity to protect the lender's position, the lender may set the bid below the amount owed.

If a third party bids at least one penny over the opening bid, that party is the new owner of the property. The third party gives the auctioneer a cashier's check for the full amount of the property and the auctioneer sends the check on to the trustee. When the funds clear, the trustee issues the third-party purchaser a trustee's deed. The trustee then pays the lender the amount owed.

If a third party does not bid at the auction, the property reverts to the beneficiary and is now considered *real estate owned* (REO) on the lender's balance sheet. The lender may then sell the property and recover the amounts owed.

Due Diligence
Researching the Investment

Now that you are familiar with the terms and concepts used in lending and the operation of mortgage pools, you are ready to learn about how to research the investment, commonly referred to as "due diligence."

Due diligence will vary based on the type of entity you are investigating and the type of license under which the entity operates.

Following are some basic due-diligence guidelines that will help you make an investment decision. Remember, there is no "standard" for what a mortgage pool can or cannot do. One fund may exclusively invest in shopping-center loans and another may invest in manufactured home loans. It is your job to comprehensively understand what you are investing in and understand the underlying associated risks.

If there is one piece of advice you should take away from reading this book, it is **read the offering memorandum.** The offering memorandum sets forth the guidelines by which the company operates. Every offering memorandum is different, and it is critical to understand how the company in which you invest will operate and compensate you.

The Offering Memorandum

Carefully read the offering memorandum (offering). This sounds basic, but in my experience, few people read the offering. Every offering is unique. The company is directed to conduct business in the manner described in the offering. The offering memorandum is the one document that all mortgage pools have in common. They may not all look exactly the same, but they contain the same basic information.

Investor Suitability

Determine if you are suited for the investment according to the guidelines in the offering. If you do not meet the guidelines, do not invest. If a member of the company is coaxing you to indicate on a subscription agreement that you do qualify, even though you know you do not, you should think about in what other ways the company may be dishonest. If you do not qualify under the described investor suitability guidelines, do not invest.

Term of the offering

What is the term of the investment? If investors may not withdraw cash early, how does the fund liquidate at maturity? Many investments of this nature are five to ten years, and after that investors may be able to vote to extend the term even longer.

Liquidity

If you wanted to redeem your shares and liquidate your investment, how would you do it? Is there a fee connected with an early withdrawal? If early withdrawals are permitted, on what reasonable time basis does the fund honor liquidity withdrawals? How much liquid cash reserves does the fund maintain in any given month? Can you afford to have your invested capital tied up for the entire term of the offering? If you cannot wait the entire term for your funds, you may want to reconsider the investment or consider investing less money.

Sales Commission

A sales commission, sometimes referred to as a "load," is paid to a broker/dealer or financial advisor at the time you purchase the investment. If the mortgage pool you are considering has a sales commission, it is usually disclosed on the front page of the offering.

If there is no sales commission, inquire as to whether or not the manager of the mortgage pool or any of its affiliates will receive a commission or fee upon your initial investment.

Sales commissions may dilute the return. For example, if you invest $100,000 and a securities broker is paid a 3 percent commission, then only $97,000 of your money is earning interest. In some cases, the manager of the fund may pay the commission on your behalf, or the commission could come from the income earned in the fund. In any case, find out if there is a commission and how it affects your investment.

First Month's Interest

Some funds will invest your money and not pay interest on the first month, or may only start accruing interest at the beginning of the month after you invest. This method will dilute you first year's yield. The investment may still be acceptable, but understand your first year's yield before you invest.

Lending Standards

What guidelines will the pool use to make loans? Understand the loan-to-value ratio, debt-to-income ratio, type of properties, priority of loans, title and casualty insurance requirements, and real estate valuation requirements.

Leverage

Leverage is the process of using debt to finance loans to increase yield. The yield increases by the difference between the cost of the debt and the return on the loans used to finance the debt. For example, assume that a fund had $20 million in loans and was able to obtain a $10 million loan (50 percent leverage) at 7 percent interest. Now assume that the fund used the $10 million in leverage to originate and/or purchase loans yielding 11 percent. The fund would increase its yield by approximately 2 percent (11 percent return on the loans, less the 7 percent cost to borrow the funds = 4 percent increased return x 50 percent leverage = 2 percent overall increased return). Find out if leverage is used. If leverage is used, how much? Leverage will boost your return under normal conditions but could cause you to lose more if loans default and the fund cannot recover the asset in a foreclosure.

If you are investing funds from an IRA or pension plan, you may be subject to UBTI (Unrelated Business Taxable Income) and could jeopardize your tax-deferred status if it is not reported properly. (See section on ERISA and IRAs for more details.)

Compensation to Managers

How is the pool manager compensated? Are there annual or monthly fees, and if so, how much? You want your fund manager to earn money and make a profit, so long as the incentives between you are aligned.

Aligned incentives mean that when the investor makes money, the fund manager makes money. For example, one fund may reward the manager a percentage return over a given benchmark, whereas another fund may always pay the manager regardless of a benchmark return. In the former case, incentives are more aligned, because the pool manager only earns a return after the investor achieves a stated benchmark return. In the latter case, incentives are not as aligned, because the manager is earning a return regardless of the fund's performance.

Origination Fees

When a loan is originated, the borrower typically pays a fee to the company originating the loan. Understand whether or not the fund shares in origination fees, or how origination fees are otherwise accounted for.

Servicing Fees

After a loan is originated, it must be serviced. Servicing is the process of collecting money from the borrower and managing delinquent accounts. Servicing fees will vary based on the underlying asset. For example, higher-quality borrowers require fewer collection phone calls and delinquency management, so the cost of servicing is lower. Poor credit borrowers typically require substantial "hand holding" and are more expensive to service. Servicing can range between 1 and 4 percent of the principal balance of a loan.

The advertised return to investors should always be the net of the servicing and other fees.

Ancillary Fees

Mortgages often have other fees included such as late fees, early termination fees, prepayment penalties, and default interest rates. Each pool is unique in regards to what fees the manager receives and what fees the pool receives. Ancillary fees increase yields.

Expenses

What expenses are paid directly from the mortgage pool? Is the pool paying for expenses such as rent, utilities, and staffing? Understand how the pool determines what is paid by the pool and what is paid by the manager.

Accounting

What are the accounting requirements? How often is the fund reviewed by an outside auditor? How often are reports made available to the shareholders?

Manager

The skill set of the pool manager will vary based on the type of entity chosen for the mortgage pool. For example, a pool that specializes in commercial lending should have a manager that has experience in commercial lending. Understand who the manager is, what experience the manager has, and what conflicts the manager may disclose about the pool and other activities in which the manager is engaged. Often times, the manager will be another entity as opposed to an individual. Ask the company who owns and runs the manager's entity and with what other entities he/it may be affiliated.

Structure

Mortgage pools exist within an entity structure. The structure may or may not have tax consequences to you, but you need to know the structure and work with your tax accountant to understand the implications of the structure. Typically, the mortgage pool exists as a Limited Liability Company (LLC), a limited partnership, or a corporation. The type of entity will determine the type of reporting on your taxes.

The structure of the entity can have a significant impact on your ability to file your tax returns. For example, if the entity is a LLC or a limited partnership, you will receive a K-1 "Partner's Share of Income, Deductions, Credits," etc. Many novice pool investors think they just receive a 1098 mortgage interest statement by January 31, and they use that to file their personal tax returns. As a shareholder of a LLC or a limited partnership, for example, you will receive a shareholder distribution report that may not be sent to you until the entity completes its tax return. This report could be at the conclusion of all IRS extension-to-file deadlines.

Most investors want their K-1s well before April so they may file their tax returns. Providing K-1s early in the year requires a significant amount of advanced planning by the company. Ask what you will receive to supplement your tax filing, and ask when you will receive it. Find out when the entity will distribute shareholder tax documents and what the history of tax distribution document distribution has been.

Corporations that elect REIT status issue 1099-DIV by the end of January, and are not subject to the K-1 challenges.

Minimum Investment

Determine the minimum initial investment and determine if that level is suitable for your objectives. Find out what additional minimum investment is required for future investments. Most fund managers have the ability to make an exception to the minimum investment level. If you are not comfortable investing the minimum amount, or do not have the minimum amount liquid at the time you would like to invest, ask if an exception can be made.

Reinvest earnings

Find out if you can reinvest earnings in the company. If you can, and you do not need the monthly cash flow, I would strongly recommend reinvesting them.

Typically companies have minimum investment requirements (e.g. $50,000, or $5,000 increments after the initial investment). Reinvesting earnings allows you to continuously reinvest a small amount of capital into the company.

CAUTION: If you reinvest your earnings, you do not receive the cash from the company. However, you will be responsible for the taxes on the dividend, unless the shares are held by a tax-deferred entity (e.g. an IRA). For example, if you are in the 25 percent combined tax and federal tax bracket and earn $10,000 in distributions, and you reinvest all the distributions that year, you would still have to pay $10,000 x 25 percent = $2,500 in combined state and federal taxes.

Business Risks

Offerings will have a section on each of the risks that the manager perceives in the business. Read this section carefully and determine if these risks are acceptable. Returns in mortgage pools are higher because the risks are higher and the funds are less liquid than in a publicly traded security. Understand the risks and be sure to diversify your own portfolio to minimize risks.

Entity and Licensing Research

Depending on the type of entity, use these guidelines to research various aspects of the company.

License Check for DRE Lenders

If the company is originating loans using a Department of Real Estate (DRE) license, you should check the status of the licensee at *http://www.dre.ca. gov/licstats.htm*. If the licensee is not active, ask why not. Investigate any past disciplinary actions and get explanations in writing.

Department of Corporations Securities Permit

If the offering is a state-regulated offering in California, it is governed by the California Department of Corporations Securities Division. This division has an electronic document management system for all correspondence with permitted entities. The system is called California Electronic Access to Securities Information (Cal-EASI) and can be accessed from the securities regulation web section at *http://www.corp.ca.gov/srd/security.htm*.

Companies issued permits by this agency are required to submit all advertisements for approval. You can get a sense of the company's compliance in this regard, or lack thereof, by the requests submitted and approved. If you do not see any written approval requests, inquire as to why you do not see them in the database. If you responded to an advertisement, find out if that advertisement was approved. If the company is not in compliance with advertising, consider in what other ways the company may not be in compliance.

Department of Corporations
CFL or RML

If the business is operating with a California Finance Lender's (CFL) or a Residential Mortgage Lender (RML) license, you may check the status of the license at the Department of Corporations Financial Services Division at *http://www.corp.ca.gov/fsd/lic.*

This site provides only limited information, including the company name, date of filing, office address, and status of the license. If the license is not "active," ask a company representative why it is no longer active and under what license they are originating loans.

Securities and Exchange Commission (SEC)

If a company is approved as a Reg D offering, or as a fully registered offering, you can find information about the company's filing using the SEC's Electronic Data Gathering, Analysis, and Retrieval system (EDGAR). EDGAR performs automated collection, validation, indexing, acceptance, and forwarding of submissions by companies and others who are required by law to file forms with the SEC. Its primary purpose is to increase the efficiency and fairness of the securities market for the benefit of investors, corporations, and the economy by accelerating the receipt, acceptance, dissemination, and analysis of time-sensitive corporate information filed with the agency.[1]

EDGAR may be accessed at: http://www.sec.gov/edgar/searchedgar/companysearch.html

Reg D offerings will have limited information because of the nature of the limited offering.

Fund Management Reports

Find out how often the pool reports activities about the underlying assets. Ask to see the past six months of reports and review them for information. Determine if the pool has more than five hundred investors and exceeds $10 million in equity. If the fund does exceed this standard, the pool will be subject to 1934 SEC Act reporting, or SEC Reg AB, reporting enacted in December 2005 by the SEC. In

---

1.   Definition from the sec.gov website: *http://www.sec.gov/edgar/aboutedgar.htm.*

either case, determine if the fund has planned for increased accounting costs in light of increased accounting regulation and whether/how they anticipate that will affect current investor returns. (See *http://www.sec.gov/rules/final/33-8518.pdf.*)

Internet Search

Perform an Internet search, using *www.google.com* or another search site, on the company and its managers and/or affiliates. Note anything significant that comes up and ask the person handling inquiries for the company about it.

Better Business Bureau

The Better Business Bureau has local chapters that handle complaints about registered businesses. To find a local chapter, go to *http://www.bbb.org,* find your local chapter, and then search by business.

Notice if the company you are investing in is a member. If the company is not a member, ask why not. Companies that belong subscribe to a set of standards regarding business conduct. Complaints in and of themselves are not necessarily cause for alarm, but inquire as to the nature of the complaint and the resolution, if any.

Underwriting Guidelines

Written underwriting guidelines give employees clear guidance on how to underwrite loans that fit the mortgage pool criteria. Find out if underwriting guidelines exist in a written form and ask to review them. Guidelines are considered confidential because they may contain sensitive screening information that the company does not want competitors to review. You should be able to review the guidelines at the office of the company, but you most likely will not receive them in an email.

Staff

Guidelines and policies are only as good as the people following them. Ask about the qualifications of the senior management team, the underwriters, and the operations staff. Staff members should be experienced in loan operations, underwriting and accounting.

Actual Pool Return

The stated mortgage pool return may be supplemented by the manager. Returns can be supplemented in two ways.

The first way to supplement returns is for the manager to forgo fees to which they would otherwise be entitled under the offering memorandum or operating agreement. For example, the manager may be entitled to a servicing fee of 1 percent, but in practice is not taking the fee. This would have the effect of boosting yields to the fund by 1 percent.

Another way returns may be supplemented by a manager is for the manager to add fees to the pool that are not included in the offering. For example, a pool may consist of first mortgages yielding 11 percent, but the pool is yielding 12 percent. The boost in yield may come from the manager sharing loan origination fees, or from sharing fees obtained by selling loans at a premium on the secondary market.

Inquire whether or not the manager is taking all of the fees disclosed in the offering memorandum. If the manager is foregoing fees now, find out how it will affect the pool's yield if the manager later takes the total disclosed fees.

In addition, some managers supplement returns by including premiums obtained from secondary market loan sales. Find out if these premiums shared with the pool are a regular part of the pools returns. If not, determine what the pool would yield without these returns.

Delinquency

What is the expected and actual delinquency rate of the fund? Delinquency can be defined in many ways. Typically, a loan is considered "late" if it is more than 10 days past due, and "delinquent" if it is thirty days past due. Ask for a breakdown of delinquent loans in the 30, 60, 90 and greater than 120 days categories. Delinquent loans are not necessarily a negative indicator. Delinquencies often provide extra profit to mortgage pool investors in the form of late fees if allocated that way in the offering memorandum. Look for trends in the delinquencies. Are delinquencies on the rise? If so, how does the fund compensate for cash flow shortages created by the delinquencies? Examine the fund's delinquency rate in comparison with other comparable industry averages.

Reserves

There are no regulatory guidelines for managing mortgage pool reserves. However, a well-managed mortgage pool should maintain several different levels of reserves.

Delinquency Reserve

A set-aside of a certain amount of cash to pay distributions of earnings to investors, even when borrowers are not making payments on time to the pool. Interest on delinquent loans should be accrued only if there is sufficient equity in the underlying property. Independent auditors should make decisions about sufficient equity and indicate whether or not certain loans should be written off as losses.

Liquidity Reserve

Cash set-aside to accommodate investor withdrawal requests.

Advance Reserve

Cash set-aside used to advance legal fees or mortgage payments that the borrower does not pay on a more senior lien.

Loan Loss and Legal Reserve

Cash set-aside and listed as an asset on the balance sheet to compensate for unexpected loan losses or legal fees relating to the mortgage pool. Find out how much, if any, is being set aside for this type of reserve.

Line of Credit Reserve

If the mortgage pool offers home equity lines of credit, determine the type of cash reserve it maintains to fulfill borrower credit line draw requests.

Error and Omissions Insurance

Error and omissions (E&O) insurance is available to mortgage originators to protect them from unexpected or unintended liability. The coverage also provides a fidelity bond to guard against employee theft. Typical coverage required by wholesale lending institutions is $300,000. Investigate whether the mortgage pool has an E & O policy, and what amount of coverage is maintained.

Third Party Origination Quality Control Policy

Many loan originators offer their loan products through a *third party* wholesale system. A third party is considered a broker/loan officer who works with the borrower to submit the loan to the mortgage pool or affiliate on behalf of the borrower. A strong third party quality-control policy details the process by which brokers and loan officers submitting loans to the company for funding are screened and audited. Items that should be covered by a comprehensive policy include:

Management of Licenses

A license-management system should be in place to determine the type of license a submitting third party has, when the license expires, and whether or not the third party has any license infractions.

File Audits

The policy should outline a systematic approach to auditing submitted files and appraisals on property submitted by third parties.

Fraud

A system should exist to detect and monitor transactions for fraud. The policy should have a monitoring procedure to screen out third parties who have submitted problem loans, or who have submitted loans which have not performed as expected.

Software and Systems

Find out what type of software and systems the pool manager has in place to manage the underlying assets and investor pool returns. Good software and systems allow the company to manage the flow of cash from loan origination through investor distribution.

Diversification

Determine the diversification of assets in the pool. Diversification reduces "concentration risk." Just as you diversify your personal portfolio to minimize risk, so too should the fund diversify its portfolio in the following areas.

Loan Amount—What is the average loan amount outstanding? What is the largest single loan outstanding, and what percentage of the pool is it? If the pool is $10 million, and there are two $5 million loans, the pool is not well diversified. If there is $10 million, and there are dozens of loans of different sizes, the pool is better diversified.

Geographic Location—Where are the underlying properties located? Are they all in one area? If all the loans are in San Francisco, for example, the pool would not be well diversified geographically vs. a pool that has assets throughout California or throughout the country.

Number of Loans—How many loans are outstanding? Are there many large loans, or several small loans, or a mix? The more loans in the fund, the more diversified it is. It is better not to have all the proverbial eggs in one basket.

References

Ask for personal and/or professional references. Understandably, many pools will not give personal investor references, because investors in the pool do not want to be bombarded with prospective investor calls. But you should be able to get business references to call and possibly one or two investor references to verify how the pool conducts business.

Visit the Office

If possible, visit the main office of the pool manager. Seeing the operations first-hand will give you insight into both the staff that manages the day-to-day operations of the pool and the underlying assets.

Attorneys, Accountants, and Financial Advisors

Consult legal counsel, your accountant, and/or a financial advisor before you invest. There are many issues that may affect you, and it is important to understand them before you invest.

In addition to helping you conduct your due diligence, here are four significant issues with which your team of professionals can assist:

Active vs. Passive Income

Mortgage pools are considered "active" income, and income from these pools may not be used to write off passive losses.

Contrary to logic, the income earned from a mortgage pool is not "passive" income. Typically, active income is income derived from a business or activity in which you actively participate. Most investors believe that since they do not participate in the management of the pool, the income derived from the pool should be passive.

The IRS, however, includes in the definition for active income "...interest income on loans and investments made in the ordinary course of a trade or business or lending money." The IRS rules also indicate that passive-activity income does not include portfolio income. Interest from a mortgage pool-type organization is considered portfolio income, and therefore it must not be treated as passive income.

For more specific information on active vs. passive income, direct your accountant or financial planner to "paragraph M-5329" of the "Federal Tax Coordinator 2d" and IRS Regulation 1.469-2T.

Lawsuits

Have your attorney research lawsuits against the name of the entity, the pool manager, the pool manager and any name affiliated with the fund, or past funds operated by the same manager.

The existence of one or more lawsuits does not necessarily mean anything. But you should ask about the lawsuits, obtain a copy of them, and understand the implication to the investment.

Audit

Ask your accountant to review the financials and financial footnotes of the company, and have them explain any positive or negative findings. Recent financials should be made available to you prior to investing.

Not all entities are required to provide audited financials. California Department of Corporations mortgage pools are required to provide annually audited statements, but Reg D companies are not. The rules and regulations vary widely surrounding audits and depend on the specific type of entity, the number of investors, and the amount of equity in the company.

Companies reporting under the 1934 Securities and Exchange Act are required to submit audited financials in accordance with the Sarbanes-Oxley Act. If the entity is an "Asset-Based Security," it falls within newly enacted SEC reporting regulations referred to as "Reg AB," and the company is not required to submit audited financials. However, the accounting firm submitting financials must be specially registered with the SEC's Public Accounting Oversight Board (PAOB) and must include an attestation with regards to servicing standards and other reporting specifically designed by asset-backed securities.

Sarbanes-Oxley and Reg AB are both complicated and far-reaching. For more information about Sarbanes-Oxley, see *http://www.sarbanes-oxley.com/*. For more information on the SEC's Reg AB, see *http://www.sec.gov/rules/final/33-8518.pdf.*

Employee Retirement Income Security Act (ERISA) and IRAs.

Many funds allow ERISA money into the pool. The Employee Retirement Income Security Act of 1974 (ERISA) contains strict fiduciary responsibility rules governing the actions of "fiduciaries" of employee benefit plans. ERISA funds include corporate pension or profit-sharing plans, or other employee benefit plans that are subject to ERISA. In any such case, the person making the investment decision concerning the purchase of Shares will be a "fiduciary" of such a plan and will be required to conform to ERISA's fiduciary responsibility rules.

IRAs are not covered under ERISA, but are subject to similar rules under Internal Revenue Code Section 4975, which includes IRA plans under Internal Revenue Code Section 408.

The rules for ERISA and IRAs are complex. I would urge you to consult your tax or pension consultant to determine the application of ERISA to your prospective investment.

The manager of a pool should not accept subscriptions for shares from ERISA plan investors unless, immediately after any such Shares are sold, the aggregate of ERISA plan investors will hold less than 25 percent of the total outstanding equity interests in the company (measured by capital accounts).

Find out what methods the pool has to manage their ERISA shareholder percentage. If the shares are mismanaged, the tax-deferred status of your entire ERISA plan could be at risk.

Owning Mortgages vs. Investing in a Mortgage Pool

Investors looking at mortgage pools often question whether or not they should own and/or service individual mortgages vs. investing in mortgage pools.

Owning mortgages will often return higher yields, but it is not for everyone. The following information will help you decide whether owning notes is right for you.

Use the following issues as a discussion point with your accountant, attorney, and/or financial advisor. Individual circumstances vary, and you will not be able to render a decision based solely on the information provided herein.

The following issues (i.e., cash flow, advances, reserves, etc.) are followed by a discussion of how the issue is typically addressed by a mortgage pool (pool) vs. how the issue is managed if you were to own an individual note (owning).

Cash Flow

Cash flow is the income you receive from the investment. As it relates to mortgages, cash flow is typically interest, late fees, and any other charges allowed according to the terms of the note or deed of trust.

Pool

A mortgage pool typically pays investors interest at regular intervals (e.g. monthly or quarterly) even when borrowers do not pay on time. To compensate for delinquent loans, the pool will maintain a reserve. If the delinquency rate is severe enough, the pool may not have adequate reserves to pay regular distributions.

Owning

Interest received from the borrower is paid to you. If the borrower does not pay, you will not receive income. The interest income will accrue, and may eventually be paid when the borrower cures a delinquency provided that there is adequate equity remaining in the property. If the borrower pays a loan servicer, the loan servicer will deduct a fee prior to sending you the funds.

Accrued Interest

Pools are typically operated on an accrual-basis accounting method. This means that income is recognized when it is earned and not when it is received. For example, if a loan generates $500/month in interest income, the $500 is recognized as income each month whether the borrower pays it or not. If the borrower does not pay the loan, the interest is "accrued" and recognized as income on the income statement, even though the cash has not yet been received. Per Generally Accepted Accounting Principals (GAAP), a company may recognize accrued interest on its books so long as there is a reasonable chance of recovering the interest.

In the world of mortgage pools, what this means is that a pool can accrue interest so long as there is a reasonable likelihood that after the pool forecloses on the asset and sells the asset, the interest that was previously accrued may now be recognized.

Example: A borrower is delinquent on a $400,000 loan secured by a $500,000 property. The accrued interest is $3,000/month on the loan. The LTV is 80 percent, and there is $100,000 equity in the property. If the lender foreclosed upon the property and later sold the property, there would likely be a substantial amount of cash remaining to pay any accrued interest:

$500,000 sale price

(40,000) less 8 percent real estate and closing fees to sell the property

(400,000) repay original principal balance on the loan

$60,000 net funds remaining to pay accrued interest.

Theoretically, the interest could accrue for $60,000 (net funds remaining after the sale)/$3,000 month (monthly interest due) = twenty months of accrued interest paid for from net funds after the sale of a foreclosed asset.

If the borrower was delinquent for twenty-five months, in this scenario, the pool would recapture twenty months of payments and lose five months of payments.

In this same scenario, as the value of the home decreased from $500,000 to $425,000, there would be no equity remaining after a sale, and therefore the pool could not accrue any interest.

$425,000 sale price

(34,000) less 8 percent real estate and closing fees to sell the property

(400,000) repay original principal balance on the loan

_____

$(9,000) net funds remaining to pay accrued interest are <u>negative.</u>

When net funds are negative, the pool should not accrue interest and should recognize a loss of $9,000 until the asset is sold and the exact loss/gain is known.

When to accrue or not accrue interest on a loan is a determination that should be made by a pool manager and confirmed by an independent accountant.

Pool

A mortgage pool that is on the accrual basis of accounting will accrue interest and pay investors whether or not the pool receives cash from the borrower, so long as the pool maintains adequate reserves and the pool's manager and auditors confirm there is sufficient collateral of the underlying delinquent loans.

Owning

You will receive cash only when the borrower pays you.

Advances

Advances take many forms. Lenders in junior positions (e.g. a second mortgage) will often advance delinquent payments to the senior lender to prevent a foreclosure. If the borrower files bankruptcy or takes any other legal action against the mortgage holder, an advance must be made to remedy the situation. Advances may also be required to pay a trustee and related fees in order to foreclose on a property.

Advances exist in the normal course of busness for loans which are revolving lines of credit. For example, if a borrower has a $100,000 line of credit and has only drawn down $80,000 of it, there is an outstanding $20,000 liability. This liability may be drawn upon by the borrower, provided the borrower meets the obligations in the note and deed of trust.

With regard to both pools and individual mortgages, advances are typically allowed to be added to the debt owed by the borrower, and interest may accrue on those advances. In the event the property does not have sufficient collateral to support the advances, these advances may not be recoverable, and therefore interest would not accrue.

Pool

Advances are typically paid for by a pool. Interest accrues on advances as guided by the note and deed of trust and is paid to investors on a regular basis as if the loan were performing.

Owning

Advances, including line-of-credit draws, legal fees, foreclosure fees, etc., are paid by the owner of the note.

Reserves

Reserves are cash set aside to manage loan losses, unexpected legal expenses, or borrower line-of-credit draws.

Pool

A well-managed pool will maintain a loan loss and legal reserve fund against which loses are booked before losses or legal fees would affect investors. Funds keep some cash liquid at all times for various advances.

Owning

A loss on any loan is a direct loss to the owner of the mortgage. Legal expenses incurred may or may not be recoverable to a note holder.

Diversification

Diversified portfolios are typically less risky than keeping all the proverbial eggs in one basket.

Pool

As a pool shareholder, you own a share of the pool and not a share of any one particular loan. Your investment is diversified across all the loans in the pool. Of course your diversification is only as good as the pool's diversification.

Owning

There is little diversification unless you own a wide variety of loans on properties in a variety of geographic locations.

Liquidity

Liquidity is the availability of cash, or the ability to obtain it quickly upon demand.

Pool

Each pool will have its own liquidity guidelines. Typically, you can redeem shares with advance notice. Some funds may charge an early-withdrawal penalty. There is usually no guarantee that the shares can be redeemed.

Owning

Liquidity is typically achieved when the note pays off or the note is sold. In rare instances investors can obtain a loan against an owned performing note, but it is uncommon, difficult and expensive.

Vesting

Vesting refers to the legal method in which the loan is titled.

Pool

Loans are vested in the name of the pool of which the investor is a shareholder.

Owning

Loans are vested in the name of the owner.

Servicing

Servicing refers to the management of the note. Collecting funds, advancing fees when necessary, interfacing with the trustee, re-conveying the note after it paid off, and providing reinstatement and payoff statements when required.

Pool

Loans are serviced by the pool itself or a company designated by the pool. Servicing costs vary, but usually range between 1 and 4 percent depending on the type of note, the type of borrower, and the amount of the note.

Owning

Owners are responsible for servicing the loan and/or paying for the servicing of the loan.

Executive Summary

Investing in a mortgage pool can be rewarding. Give the investment careful consideration and conduct the due diligence that is commensurate with the investment you are making.

Here is a review of the most important considerations before you invest.

Read the offering memorandum. The offering memorandum is the guide for the pool and the criteria for the origination and purchasing of the underlying assets.

Determine the type of pool and required licensing. Know the type of legal entity for the investment and the type of licensing required to raise funds and conduct business.

Consult your financial and legal advisors. Make sure the investment is in line with your overall financial objectives and that you are properly qualified to make the investment.

Conduct Due Diligence. Use the techniques presented in this book to research the pool manager, the company, the underlying loans, and underwriting guidelines. Make sure that the investment risks are acceptable risks to you before you invest.

You can earn higher yields in today's low-yield world. But like everything else in life, higher yields are achieved with additional effort. Use the knowledge and insights in this book to begin evaluating mortgage pools for your portfolio today, and earn higher yields tomorrow.

Author Bio

Martin I. Goodman was born and raised in Cleveland, Ohio, and moved to San Diego, California, in 1986, where he now resides. Martin has over fifteen years experience as a business entrepreneur including direct sales, marketing, and systems development. He is founder of Residential Capital Mortgage Income Fund LLC (www.ResCapFunds.com) and the Managing Member of the Residential Capital Alliance Fund, LP. Prior to operating his mortgage pools, Martin was in real estate re-development where he purchased and resold more than 500 residential properties for his various businesses.

He is a graduate of Miami University (Oxford, OH), where he graduated Magna Cum Laude in 1984 with a B.S. in Business, and he earned an MBA from the University of San Diego in 1997, graduating Valedictorian of his class. He holds a California Department of Real Estate Broker's License, California Finance Lender Licenses (#603-9040, 603-9041, 603-9039, 603-9952), and California Department of Corporations Securities Permit (#309-3236).

He is an active member of several organizations, including the California Mortgage Association, the California Association of Mortgage Brokers, the California Association of Realtors, and the Mortgage Bankers Association,

Martin is an active philanthropist and founded the non-profit 'Residential Capital Foundation' which supports youth and families in need.

To learn more about investing in the Residential Capital Mortgage Income Fund, please visit *www.ResCapFunds.com* or call (866) 235-4872.

Martin is always striving to improve upon the information provided in this book. If you have additional information, corrections, clarifications, or enhancements you would like to see included in the next edition, please feel free to email him at earninghighyield@rescap.biz.

978-0-595-39084-7
0-595-39084-6